WILLIAM HOWARD TAFT

PRESIDENT AND CHIEF JUSTICE

Mark P. Painter

JARNDYCE & JARNDYCE PRESS
CINCINNATI BOOK PUBLISHERS

Acknowledgments

Many thanks to the National Park Service staff of the William Howard Taft National Historic Site, especially Eric Patterson, Ray Henderson, and Kevin McMurry, for the fine collection of photographs. Seth Taft (grandson of William Howard) and his wife, Franny Taft, shared their research and were good enough to review the draft.

Editor: Mary E. Hull
Production: Cincinnati Book Publishing
Printed by John S. Swift Co., Inc., Cincinnati, OH

Library of Congress Control Number: 2004096631

ISBN 0-972-1916-2-3 paperback
ISBN 0-972-1916-4-x library edition

Cover: *William Howard Taft, 1909*, by Joaquin Sorolla y Bastida. Oil on canvas, (150 x 80 cm.) Taft Museum of Art, Cincinnati, Ohio. Lent by the estates of Louise Taft Semple and Jane Taft Ingalls. President Taft sat for this painting April 6–12, while he was in the White House. It was commissioned by his brother Charles Phelps Taft.

To purchase additional books, visit www.cincybooks.com.

CONTENTS

Of all his accomplishments, Taft was proudest of his service as chief justice of the Supreme Court from 1921–1930.

1

CHIEF JUSTICE

In October of 1929, chief justice of the United States William Howard Taft, who had just turned seventy-two in September, waited to go out on the Supreme Court bench to hear some of his final cases. His health was failing, and he had decided to resign soon. He did not want the work of the Court to suffer because of his physical inability to write decisions explaining the rulings in its cases.

The United States Supreme Court is the highest court in the country. It is an appellate court, which means that there are no trials held there. Instead, the nine justices review what happened in the trial courts and lower appellate courts, and they decide whether any mistakes were made. After the Supreme Court justices make a decision, one of them writes up the decision to explain their ruling. Taft had always liked the writing part of being a judge.

Taft had been chief justice for nine years. But he had been a judge before. From 1887 to 1890 he was a trial-court judge in Cincinnati, Ohio, his hometown. From 1892 to 1900 he was an appellate judge on the U.S. Sixth Circuit Court of Appeals, also based in Cincinnati. In fact, as he thought back, his happiest days had been those when his life was focused on the law. Taft had always loved the law. He would have gladly stayed a judge in Cincinnati, but history had other plans for him.

When he was a young man growing up in Cincinnati, going to Yale College, and then Cincinnati Law School, Taft assumed he would always be a lawyer or a judge. He never would have guessed where his life would take him. It was a long and varied career. He had been solicitor general of the United States—the chief lawyer for the U.S. government in the Supreme Court. He had been the first dean of the University of Cincinnati College of Law. He had supervised the construction of the Panama Canal. He even went halfway around the world to be the first American governor of the Philippine Islands after the United States took over this territory following the Spanish-American War. He had also been secretary of war under President Theodore Roosevelt and a professor of law at Yale.

As chief justice of the Supreme Court, Taft felt he had accomplished much. When he took office in 1921, the federal judicial system was a mess. There was a shortage of judges. Cases took forever to be heard, even in the Supreme Court. The rules of procedure were outdated. In his nine years as chief justice, Taft had reformed the federal judiciary. He would leave the Supreme Court, and all the federal courts, much better and more modern than they were when he started.

Taft felt a sense of accomplishment from his work on the Supreme Court. As he reflected on his career, he remembered the Philippines, Panama, family life in Cincinnati, and Yale. Another memory crept in: the fearsome Cincinnati Courthouse riot of 1884, when an angry mob, protesting the outcome of a murder trial, had burned the courthouse to the ground. These were the memories that first came to mind.

Lastly, he remembered that he had also been president of the United States.

2

GROWING UP
IN CINCINNATI

William Howard Taft, known as a child as "Willie" was born on September 15, 1857, in Cincinnati, Ohio. Cincinnati was then known as the "Queen City of the West."

The Tafts were originally a New England family. The first Taft in America, Robert Taft, emigrated from England and first settled in Braintree, Massachusetts. He was a carpenter, and a "plain, unlettered man."[1] He later moved to Mendon, Massachusetts, where he served on the board of selectmen, a village council. Thus began the Taft family tradition of public service. One of his and his wife, Sarah's, children was Joseph, who married Elizabeth Emerson. Ralph Waldo Emerson, the famous nineteenth-century writer, was indirectly descended from this family.

Joseph and Elizabeth's grandson was Aaron Taft, William Howard Taft's great-grandfather. He moved to

A young William Howard Taft, age one, and his mother, Louise Torrey Taft.

the small village of Townshend, Vermont. His son, Peter Rawson Taft, was a state representative in Vermont, continuing the Taft tradition of public service. Their son, William Howard Taft's father, Alphonso Taft, was born in Townshend in 1810.

Farm life was not for Alphonso. After teaching school for a while, he got his law degree from Yale College in 1838. He then decided that he should leave New England and find a place to settle down and practice law. He first went to New York City, but he found the lawyers there too concerned with making money. Although Alphonso wanted to make money, he believed that money was not a goal in itself. Money only allowed a person to live well and raise a family. He then traveled to Philadelphia, where he found the lawyers much more to his liking. But because there were many lawyers in Philadelphia, he thought he might have trouble making a start there.

Cincinnati was Alphonso's next stop. Though today Cincinnati does not seem very far "west," it was considered a western city in the first half of the nineteenth century because the country had not yet expanded much farther. Cincinnati was also the sixth-largest city in the United States at that time. Only New York, Baltimore, New Orleans, Philadelphia, and Boston had more people. Cincinnati, it seemed to Alphonso, had a lot of law business, but very few good lawyers.[2] He thought he could make a good living there.

Alphonso Taft moved to Cincinnati in 1838. He opened a law office and proceeded to his next goal, finding a wife. Alphonso was not a romantic man, but a practical one. He thought that marriage was the only proper status for a young lawyer because being married showed stability and seriousness. He settled on Fanny Phelps, a young woman who was the daughter of the judge in his hometown.

Alphonso married Fanny Phelps on August 29, 1841. She was just eighteen; he was thirty-one. They had two children who lived past childhood—Charles Phelps Taft and Peter Rawson Taft. But Fanny died in 1852, leaving Alphonso a widower with two young children. He believed he had to find another wife if the children were to be properly bought up and cared for.

About eighteen months after Fanny's death, Alphonso married Louise Torrey, whom he had met during a trip back east to New England. She was twenty-six; he was forty-three. Throughout their life together, she called her husband "Mr. Taft."[3] Louise immediately became a loving stepmother to young Charles Phelps Taft and Peter Rawson Taft (called Rossy).

Many children at that time died very young, and Alphonso and Louise's first child, born in 1855, died a year later. Their second child was born on September 15, 1857, and was called William Howard Taft, or "Willie" for short. Two more sons, Henry and Horace, followed in 1859 and 1861. The Tafts now had five boys, and they hoped for a daughter. They got their wish in 1865 when Frances Louise Taft was born.

Taft at age eleven (holding reins) with brothers Henry (on pony) and Horace.

In 1865 Alphonso left his successful law practice to become a Cincinnati judge, and he served in that position until 1872. Although he was nominated for the position by both the Republican and Democratic Parties, he was a Republican through and through. The Republican Party was relatively new then. It had been formed in 1854 by those who wanted to keep slavery from spreading in the United States. Alphonso had been a delegate to the very first Republican national convention, held in Philadelphia in 1856. That year the party nominated western explorer John C. Frémont for president. Though he did not win, he did well and paved the way for another

Taft's father, Alphonso Taft.

Republican candidate, Abraham Lincoln, who was elected president in 1860.

Alphonso was against slavery, and he was even impatient with President Lincoln for not moving fast enough to end it. Willie Taft grew up listening to his father's antislavery opinions.

The Taft family lived in a substantial house on Mt. Auburn, a close suburb of Cincinnati. The house was large, but not grand like some of the others on Auburn Avenue. In fact, it looked much like a shoebox. There was a lot of land in the back, including orchards and various outbuildings.

Another nickname Willie acquired in childhood was "Big Lub." He was a large child, and later he became a large man. He had sandy hair and blue eyes. He was tall and heavy, but he played baseball regularly and was always a baseball fan. The Taft children also swam often in the canal at the bottom of the hill.

Education was one of his father's passions. Alphonso insisted that his children get as much education as possible.[4] All the Taft children attended public school in Cincinnati. "Will," as he became known as a young man, attended the old Woodward High School. It was about three-quarters of a mile from their house on Auburn Avenue. To get to school Will walked south on Auburn Avenue, then around a bend where Auburn turned into

12

This photograph of the Taft home on Auburn Avenue was taken in 1868. Henry Taft is on the pillar; Will Taft is standing at the fence.

Sycamore Street. Sycamore went steeply downhill. Will Taft would have seen new construction as he walked, for the area was growing. Walking home up the steep hill was good exercise.

Will was a model student in high school and he took college preparatory courses. There is no record of his ever getting into trouble. Back then, students received grades for their general behavior, or "deportment." Will Taft never get below 92 percent in that category.[5] He finished high school second in his class. Following family tradition, he prepared to attend Yale College.

3

THE YOUNG
LAWYER

Will Taft traveled east to attend Yale College in the fall of 1874. His father had attended the same college forty years earlier. Taft studied hard. He made many friends and was the most popular person in his class. He was frugal with the money supplied by his father and sent home accountings of each penny.[1] He did not drink hard liquor or use tobacco, though he may have had an occasional beer or glass of wine.

Taft changed his nickname from "Will" to "Bill" when he came to Yale. (He was later to change it back to Will.) He did not go out for the rowing, football, or baseball teams, because his father thought these activities would take away from study time.

In college, he was regarded as honest, upright, and a leader. He had a pleasant attitude, and was very well liked and respected. Taft's fellow students elected him

Will Taft's high school photo. After graduating second in his class, Taft traveled east to attend Yale College, his father's alma mater.

class orator, and he gave a speech at his graduation in 1878. He finished second in his class—just as he had at Woodward High School.[2]

After Yale, Taft returned to Cincinnati to become a lawyer. Unlike his father, who pursued his legal education at Yale, Taft went to Cincinnati Law School. Because his classes lasted about two hours a day, law studies took up only part of Taft's time.[3] He also worked in his father's law office part-time, though he was not as hard working as his father wanted him to be. In his father's view, Taft wasted too much time by going to races, plays, and social events.[4]

Taft's father was a busy man. He was gradually winding down his law practice because he was also serving the government in Washington, D.C. In 1876 President Ulysses S. Grant first appointed Alphonso Taft as secretary of war and then attorney general of the United States.

While still in law school, Taft obtained a paying job as a reporter for the *Cincinnati Commercial* newspaper. He was assigned to cover the courts, so he was able to see the law applied firsthand.[5] Taft decided to take the bar exam in Columbus even before he graduated from law school.[6] After reading law books in his father's office for a few weeks, he passed. Taft graduated from law school and was licensed to practice law in 1880.[7]

Taft went into public service almost immediately. In October of 1880, he was appointed an assistant county prosecuting attorney for Hamilton County—the county in which Cincinnati was located. The prosecuting attorney (in some states called a state's attorney or district attorney), was the chief legal officer for the county.

Will Taft was assigned to prosecute criminal cases, from theft to murder. He stayed only a year in this job. During this time, Taft was also doing political work—he had even been named chief election supervisor. He traveled around the state, speaking on behalf of Republican Party candidates.

Taft's political work for the Republican Party, and his father's political influence, soon got him a federal government appointment. President Chester Arthur named him collector of internal revenue for Cincinnati, and he began his duties in March 1881. Taft was only twenty-four—quite young for such a responsible position. There were many opportunities for bribery and corruption in this job, and because Taft felt that his honesty might be questioned if he remained, he held the job for only two years.[8] While collector of internal revenue for the city of Cincinnati, Taft collected taxes from distillers of whisky. The distillers were sometimes known to offer bribes in return for lower taxes. Another major problem with the position involved his fellow employees. The custom at the time was for a few real employees to do most of the work. Additional government employees were hired as favors for various Republican politicians. Will Taft did not like this waste of public money.

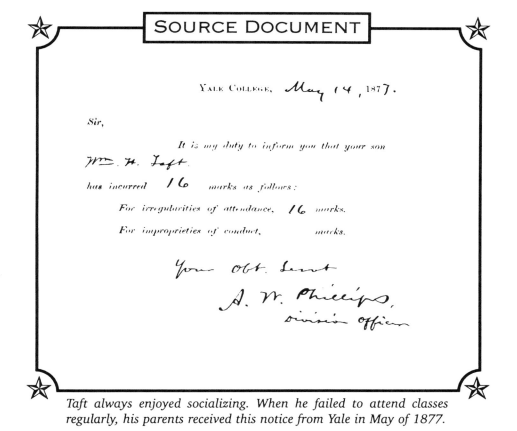

SOURCE DOCUMENT

YALE COLLEGE, *May 14, 1877.*

Sir,

It is my duty to inform you that your son

Wm. H. Taft.

has incurred *16* marks as follows:

For irregularities of attendance, *16* marks.

For improprieties of conduct, marks.

Your obt. servt

A. W. Phillips,
division officer

Taft always enjoyed socializing. When he failed to attend classes regularly, his parents received this notice from Yale in May of 1877.

Taft's years as a young bachelor were not all work. One of his friends had done legal work for the theater owners of Cincinnati, and was paid, at least partly, in theater passes. Taft and a group of young men often went to dinner and the theater together. They also went to the beer halls that lined the "Over-the-Rhine" section of Cincinnati. This section was just across the canal from downtown, and it was named for the large German immigrant population that lived there.

Though Will Taft liked to have a good time, there is no

evidence that he participated much in the drinking. He was more fond of eating and conversation. He was then just over six feet tall and carried his weight well; he was substantial rather than fat. But he certainly was not thin.

At the time, Cincinnati was ruled by the Republican Party, although the Democrats occasionally won some offices. Taft was a party worker, and he got along with the bosses of the city's Republican "machine," as it was called then. Many big cities had political machines—some were Democratic and some were Republican. The machine controlled all the public jobs in the city. Jobs were handed out more for party loyalty than for the ability to do the job. Political machines were often corrupt, but Taft did not participate in any corruption. He was scrupulously honest.

In 1883, after resigning from his position as collector of internal revenue in Cincinnati, Taft formed a law partnership with a former associate of his father. He also went abroad for the first time. It was summer, and in the oppressive heat of Cincinnati, the courts and offices closed, or at least went on an abbreviated schedule. Before the invention of air conditioning, people who could afford to travel left Cincinnati in the summer.

Taft went to Ireland, Scotland, and England. He then visited his parents at their new home in Vienna. In 1882 President Arthur had appointed Alphonso Taft the United States minister to Austria-Hungary. Today this position is known as ambassador. Taft's father would later enjoy another diplomatic position as U.S. minister to Russia.

Back home in Cincinnati, events were occurring that would have an impact on Will Taft's career. On Christmas Eve in 1883 two Cincinnati men robbed and murdered

From 1882–1884 Taft's father, seated, served as the U.S. Minister to Austria-Hungary.

their employer, a stable owner. Everyone thought the men would hang, which was the punishment then for murder. But the first man to come to trial, William Berger, had a shady lawyer whom the family had scraped together money to hire. The jury returned a verdict of guilty of manslaughter. Manslaughter was a lesser offense and saved the defendant from hanging.

The people of Cincinnati were outraged. They thought the jury had been bribed. For years, there had been rumors of jury bribing, and there were often long delays in trials. People thought the city justice system was in the control of the criminal lawyers. In March of 1884 a meeting was held as local citizens got together to protest what they thought was a corrupt court system. The meeting soon got out of hand, and a mob of angry citizens marched on the jail, which was behind the courthouse. Their intention was to take and hang Berger, but he had already been moved out of town by the sheriff. The mob burned the courthouse to the ground. In the next few days, fifty-four people were killed in the rioting. Only the arrival of the state militia, sent in by railroad from Toledo, stopped the out-of-control crowd.

After the Cincinnati Courthouse riot, Taft was named to a committee of lawyers who attempted to have Berger's lawyer, Tom Campbell, disbarred—removed as a lawyer. Taft gained much respect and favorable comment for his efforts, but Campbell was not disbarred. Another result of the fire set by the mob was that the law library in the courthouse had been lost, all but one book. Taft, as a now-prominent member of the bar, was appointed to a committee to rebuild the library's collection of law books.

In 1884, Taft campaigned for Republican Party candidates, including presidential nominee James G. Blaine. But a Democrat, Grover Cleveland, was elected president instead.

By this time, twenty-seven year old Will Taft was one of the most eligible young men in Cincinnati. He came from a distinguished family, and he was tall and good looking, if a bit overweight. Though not wealthy, he did not want for money. He was living in a fashionable new apartment building downtown, and his future was bright.

Helen "Nellie" Herron was the daughter of a prominent Cincinnati lawyer. Nellie and Will had known each other for some time, but they started seeing each other romantically in 1884. Will Taft fell madly in love. Nellie was intelligent, and like his father Alphonso, Taft liked intelligent women. She was also attractive, with brown hair and soft brown eyes. He pursued Nellie in every way he could and asked her to marry him in 1885. At first she said no, because young women of that time were supposed to decline the first several offers of marriage before finally accepting.[9]

In the spring of 1885 Nellie finally agreed to marry him, and the engagement lasted more than a year. They were married on June 19, 1886. He was twenty-eight and she was twenty-five. As a gift to the newlyweds, Nellie's parents presented them with a river-view lot in Walnut

Taft, center, sits with Helen "Nellie" Herron and friends.

Hills, the suburb just to the east of Taft's boyhood home in Mount Auburn. With Mr. Herron guaranteeing the loan, they built a home on the lot.

Nellie was well educated, and she and Taft often discussed literature and politics. It is likely that she wanted a career of her own—maybe even as a lawyer (though that was almost unheard of then)—but she transferred her ambition to her husband once they were married.[10] She would later urge him on to higher office.

Nellie's father had once taken her to the White House as a teenager, on the occasion of President and Mrs. Rutherford Hayes's twenty-fifth wedding anniversary. Her father had been a law partner with Hayes many years earlier. Nellie liked the White House, and dreamed of living there one day.

Will Taft became a judge shortly after he and Nellie married. He had campaigned for Joseph Foraker for Ohio governor in 1883 and 1885. In gratitude for Taft's help, and because Taft was highly thought of as a lawyer, Governor Foraker named him a judge of the Superior Court in Cincinnati when a vacancy arose in that position.[11] He took the office in March of 1887. Once again, Taft had gained office through political influence, but no one doubted he was well qualified. Almost all government offices at this time were gained through political influence.

William Howard Taft was now married, and a judge. He had already served as an assistant prosecuting attorney, collector of internal revenue, and he had practiced law. He was not yet thirty years old.

4

JUDGE TAFT

Will Taft was suited to being a judge. His first judgeship was on the Superior Court of Hamilton County, in Cincinnati, where Ohio Governor Joseph Foraker appointed him to a vacancy in March 1887. The superior court was a trial court, which heard all kinds of cases. Taft's father, Alphonso Taft, had once been a judge of this same court.

Will Taft had a good reputation as a lawyer, but he really had not practiced law that much. Though he had officially been a lawyer since 1880, he had mostly held government jobs. The internal revenue job, for instance, had little to do with the law. Recognizing that his legal skills needed work, Taft applied himself diligently to the judgeship. Taft had to run for election to keep his judgeship, and he was easily elected in 1888. In 1889 Will and Nellie's first son, Robert Alphonso Taft, was born.

Taft was named as an appellate judge to the United States Circuit Court for the Sixth Appellate Circuit in 1892.

While a judge of the superior court, Taft briefly had the hope of being appointed to the United States Supreme Court. Though he was very young, some important people, including Governor Foraker, were advocating his appointment to President Benjamin Harrison. Justices of the United States Supreme Court are appointed by the president, and have to be confirmed, or approved, by the Senate. They then serve for life. Taft was not appointed to the Supreme Court as he had hoped, but President Harrison did offer him the job of solicitor general of the United States. The solicitor general was under the attorney general of the United States and represented the United States government before the Supreme Court. Thus Taft would be the government's chief lawyer at the Supreme Court.

The honor was indeed great for someone so young. Taft was just thirty-two when he was sworn in. He and Nellie moved from Cincinnati to Washington, D.C., where they rented a small house.

Taft's major job as solicitor general was to prepare briefs, which are written legal papers that try to convince a court to rule a certain way. He also had to argue cases before the Supreme Court. Though he was never a great speaker, Taft's powers of speech improved somewhat by exercise.

While in Washington, Taft met Theodore Roosevelt, who was a member of the Civil Service Commission. Their destinies would intersect later. They lived close to each other and sometimes walked to work together. When fellow Ohioan William McKinley was president, Taft put in a good word for his friend Roosevelt to be appointed to a federal position. McKinley named Roosevelt assistant secretary of the navy.

Taft was solicitor general for three years. He argued twenty-seven cases before the Supreme Court and won most of them. Then Congress created the Federal Circuit Courts of Appeal. The federal courts had become slow and there was a feeling that more judges and courts were needed. The circuit courts were created to handle appeals from the trial courts.

The United States Circuit Court for the Sixth Appellate Circuit was to have its home in Cincinnati, and William Howard Taft was named one of its three judges. The court heard cases in four states—Ohio, Michigan, Kentucky, and Tennessee—so Taft would have to travel some of the time. This new court did double duty. The individual judges heard trials and motions, and the three judges together decided appeals.

Up to this point, Taft had never served for more than three years in any one job. He had been promoted regularly without much effort on his part. Later he said that even though he did not seek most of the offices he held, his "plate was right-side up"[1] when offices were handed out. That is, he was available. The country was also much smaller than it is now, and the percentage of educated people was smaller still. It also helped that Taft came from a prosperous, if not rich, family. Public office then, as now, did not pay a great amount of money. But public officials were expected to maintain a prosperous lifestyle. So it was only natural that people of the more wealthy classes were thought of first when appointive office was available—these people could afford to serve the public.

Taft was helped throughout his career by money from his family—first from his father, and later from his older brother Charles Phelps Taft. Charles was a half-brother; his mother was Alphonso's first wife. But all the Taft siblings considered themselves brothers and sister, disregarding their different mothers. Charles, as well as Nellie, always pushed Will to do more and aspire to greater things.

Taft's new position as appellate judge was his favorite so far, and he held it for eight years. During that time, beginning in 1896, he was also a law professor and the first dean of the University of Cincinnati College of Law. (His alma mater, the Cincinnati Law School, had merged with the University of Cincinnati.) In Taft's time, federal judges were not limited, as they are now, in taking jobs outside the judiciary, so it was not unusual for Taft to be head of a law school. A bronze full-size statue of William Howard Taft now stands on the grounds of the UC College of Law.

In his eight years on the circuit court, Taft wrote legal opinions in numerous cases. His rulings were clear and forceful, but his writing style was ponderous. He used too many words and wrote sentences that were too long. But that was the legal style of the day.

During Taft's time on the circuit court, changes were taking place in American industry. Working people were

Taft stands with his older brother Charles Phelps Taft I. Charles was well off and generously provided financial assistance to his younger brother.

struggling to form unions. They wanted better pay and safer working conditions. In the 1890s, major companies, controlled by a few wealthy individuals, set wages and prices. They often agreed among themselves to set low wages, and to oppose the formation of labor unions. Without unions, factory workers had no say.

Some people believed that unions were dangerous.

Taft poses with his son Charles Phelps II and daughter Helen.

They thought that the working people might become too powerful and take over the country. Most of Taft's friends and fellow judges believed that unions should be limited. That was the view of many wealthy people. Taft was, both by training and temperament, a conservative. He looked upon change with suspicion.

On the circuit court, Taft ruled against the unions when they staged a boycott—tried to prevent other companies from dealing with a company they said was unfair. Sometimes the unions would go on strike and refuse to allow their members to work for a company. The union would also tell other companies not to handle the goods of the boycotted company—or else the union members of that company would also go on strike.

In the 1890s the railroads were the most important form of transportation for goods and people in the United

States. When workers went on strike against one of the country's railroads, Judge Taft issued an injunction—a legal order forbidding the union from involving other companies in the dispute. He then jailed a union leader for violating the order. This action was not unusual at the time, but Taft did get a reputation for being anti-union. He believed in the workers' right to strike—but not to "boycott" other companies not directly involved in the dispute.

In other instances, Taft ruled on the side of working people. In the days before workers compensation laws (which provide for payment of medical bills and lost wages for those injured at work) a worker who was hurt on the job received no assistance. A legal doctrine existed called "assumption of risk." That is, if you work in a place where you know you could get hurt, your employer owes you nothing. Judge Taft ruled against this doctrine. He said that employers must make the workplace safe, or pay the bills of those workers who are hurt on the job. Taft was ahead of his time—the first workers compensation law was not passed until 1910. Workers compensation laws were eventually passed in all states.

In another case, Judge Taft sided with those who were fighting against monopolies. A monopoly exists when one company, or group of companies, is able to control prices for certain goods. The monopoly can then charge what-ever it wants to consumers. In 1890 Congress had passed the Sherman Antitrust Act, meant to make monopolies illegal, but the courts had not enforced it much. Taft wrote a decision upholding this law. He ruled against a group of companies that had gotten together to fix prices for metal pipe in the Midwest. Once again, Taft was ahead of his time on this issue, which would become even more important in future years.

While Taft was an appellate judge on the circuit court, he and Nellie had two more children—Helen, born in 1891, and Charles Phelps II (named after William's half-brother), born in 1897. The family, two boys and a girl, was now complete.

During this time Taft's older brother Charles acquired a controlling interest in the *Cincinnati Times-Star*, a major daily newspaper. He acquired money to buy the newspaper by marrying the daughter of a very rich man, David Sinton. Charles had some money of his own, and he had inherited about fifty thousand dollars from his grandfather Phelps.[2] (Will and his brothers, whose mother was Alphonso's second wife, Louise, did not have that grandfather). Charles made a great deal of money, and he was able to help his brother throughout his career.

William Howard Taft was content to be a judge and believed he would remain a judge for his career. He hoped to be elevated to the United States Supreme Court, which was the only higher court than the circuit court. But history had other plans, at least for a while.

30

GOVERNOR OF
THE PHILIPPINES

As a federal judge in Cincinnati, William Howard Taft could never have guessed that he would one day live halfway around the world and be in charge of a country he had hardly heard of. But all this happened as a result of the Spanish-American War.

"Remember the Maine" is the slogan most associated with the Spanish-American War, which began in 1898. The people of Cuba, an island in the West Indies, had long been ruled by Spain. They had rebelled against Spanish colonial rule. To protect the many Americans living in Cuba from violence between the Cuban rebels and the Spanish, the United States had sent a battleship, the U.S.S. *Maine,* to Havana in January of 1898. The ship blew up, and 266 American sailors were killed. To this day, it is not known whether the Spanish had anything to do with the explosion, but the American newspapers thought so.

Urged on by the public sentiment whipped up by the newspapers, the United States came into the war on the side of the Cuban freedom fighters. It was a short war, and the Americans defeated the Spanish easily.

During the war, Judge Taft's friend Theodore Roosevelt made himself famous by organizing the "Rough Riders," a cavalry regiment in the U.S. Army. Roosevelt led his men to an important victory in the war, and the newspapers made him a hero.

In addition to Cuba, Spain also ruled the Philippine Islands in the Pacific—halfway around the globe from the United States. During the war, The U.S. Naval Fleet attacked the Spanish in the Philippines, defeating them. As part of the settlement after the war, the United States took possession of the Philippines and became a global power for the first time.

The United States had once been a group of colonies itself. It had never before participated in the system of colonialism, in which European countries took possession of developing countries, calling them colonies.

The United States did not want a colony in the Philippines, but it took over control of the country from Spain. The Philippines were known as a "protectorate." The United States intended to "protect" the Philippine people from being taken over by another European power. The plan was for the United States to guide the Philippines to eventual independence. Also, because the United States was becoming a world power, it needed bases for its navy and army in far-off lands. The Philippines, because of its proximity to China and Japan, was ideal. Ships could be based there, and they would be close to any potential trouble spots in Asia.

Before granting the Philippines independence, the United States needed to set up a government there. The U.S. government felt that it would take many years to condition the natives to self-government and democratic ideals.

President William McKinley summoned Judge Taft to Washington. He asked him to go to the Philippines as head of a commission to decide the government of the country. Later, Taft was to take over as governor-general of the Philippines. The position would put Taft in total charge of the country.

But Taft really wanted to remain a judge. His appointment to the circuit court was for life. Knowing this, President McKinley promised Taft that if he took the Philippines position, he would be appointed to the Supreme Court when the next vacancy occurred. Nellie encouraged her husband to accept this offer, feeling this was a great opportunity to advance his career.

Taft, Nellie, Robert, Helen, and Charlie set off for the Philippines in 1900. The administration of the Philippines was under the supervision of the War Department, and the U.S. Army was in charge of the Philippines when the Tafts arrived. The army was putting down a revolt of the Philippine people. It had started against the Spanish, and now it continued against the new power, the Americans. Taft agreed that the Philippines were not ready for self-government, but he thought the army was being much too harsh.

The general in charge was Arthur MacArthur (father of the famous World War II general, Douglas MacArthur).

His policy was to conquer and rule the Philippine people. Taft, on the other hand, wanted to be friendly and teach them self-government.

With the support of President McKinley and Secretary of War Elihu Root, Taft was able to wrestle control away from the army and become governor-general of the Philippines in 1901. MacArthur was called back to the United States, and Taft was in complete charge. But the job was not easy. The Philippines consisted of many scattered islands. There were many different races, religions, and languages. While most people were very poor, there had been a ruling class, consisting mostly of Spanish property owners. The Roman Catholic Church was also part of the ruling establishment in the Philippines. It owned almost

Escolta Street in downtown Manila, Philippines, circa 1900. After President McKinley appointed Taft to the Philippine Commission in 1900, the Taft family moved to the Philippines. Taft become governor-general of the Pacific island protectorate in 1901.

four hundred thousand acres of the best land. Most people owned no land and were very poor.

Taft went to see the Pope, the leader of the Roman Catholic Church, in Rome. After lengthy negotiations, the United States purchased 390,000 acres of the church's land for over $7 million in gold. Taft distributed this land in small parcels to poor residents.

During Taft's trip to Italy he wrote Secretary of War Root that he had ridden a horse to a village in the mountains. Referring to Taft's size, Root jokingly wrote back "How is the horse?"

Taft showed that he could laugh at himself when he replied: "Your cable inquiry about the condition of the horse that brought me up the mountain was too good to keep, so I published the dispatch and have been made the subject of jokes in the local newspapers ever since."[1]

Taft's administration of the Philippines was a great success. He treated the people fairly and set up a government with a constitution modeled after the U.S. Constitution, including a Bill of Rights. The Philippine people grew to love the Tafts.

Nellie Taft was her husband's top advisor. He discussed all issues with her and often followed her advice because he respected her judgment.

President McKinley's appointment of Taft was hailed as brilliant—the newspapers and political leaders said he had picked the best person for the job. Taft's legal training was extremely useful in setting up a civil government and establishing the rule of law. Because Taft had little executive or administrative experience, there was no way to know that he would excel at managing a country. But he was an excellent leader. He learned everything he could about the land and people, and he applied his considerable talent for work to the job. Taft worked ten to twelve hours a day, despite the stifling heat.

While Taft was in the Philippines, President McKinley was reelected in 1900. Taft's old friend, Theodore Roosevelt, was his new vice president. Then McKinley was assassinated in 1901, and Roosevelt assumed the presidency. At forty-three years old, Roosevelt was the youngest president ever.

Shortly after Roosevelt took office, there was a vacancy on the Supreme Court, and Roosevelt offered Taft the position. It was what Taft had always wanted, but he had unfinished business in the Philippines. While he really wanted to be on the Supreme Court, he felt he could not accept, because he had just begun the work of restructuring the Philippines. He had to see the task through. He telegraphed President Roosevelt: "Great honor deeply appreciated, but I must decline. Situation here most critical . . . Look forward to a time I can accept."[2] That time would be very far in the future, as it turned out.

Taft's success in the Philippines brought him national attention. Newspapers praised his reforms and able administration. There was even talk of Taft becoming the Republican presidential nominee in 1904. Theodore Roosevelt planned to run in 1904, but some businessmen feared he would try to break up or "bust" the associations called trusts, which controlled many industries. And no vice president who had attained the office after a president's death had ever kept that office in the next election.

Taft did not pursue the presidency. Roosevelt, despite the misgivings of some in the Republican Party, was easily nominated.

Taft helped set up a democratic form of government in the Philippines. This photo is of the first Philippine General Assembly, circa 1907.

There was another vacancy on the Supreme Court in early 1903. Again, Roosevelt asked Taft to come home. Again Taft declined, for the same reason. He needed more time to finish his work in the Philippines. He stayed another year.

By the fall of 1903, Taft had the Philippines on a sound footing, and he believed he had accomplished his mission. He had established an education system, a government, and transportation and communication among the islands. The education system was particularly good. Hundreds of American college graduates had been recruited to come to the Philippines to teach.

Secretary of War Elihu Root told Roosevelt that he

Taft sits with Theodore Roosevelt's outgoing secretary of war, Elihu Root, whom he replaced in 1903.

would leave that office by the end of 1903. Root was a close advisor and a very effective cabinet officer. Roosevelt decided he needed an equally strong replacement. Roosevelt again asked Taft to come back to Washington, this time as secretary of war. Partly because the War Department still had charge of administering the Philippines, Taft accepted. Roosevelt told him that he would not only be a cabinet officer, but also a counselor and general troubleshooter.

In December 1903, the Tafts left the Philippines for Washington, D.C. On the way home, they stopped in Tokyo at the invitation of the Emperor of Japan. Taft had lunch and a long conversation with the emperor and many of his ministers. This was to be the first of his diplomatic missions for President Roosevelt.

SECRETARY
OF WAR

I n February of 1904, Will Taft began his job as secretary of war, a post once held by his father, Alphonso.

After spending the winter in Santa Barbara, California, Nellie joined her husband at his new post in Washington, D.C. The Tafts participated in Washington society, often dining at the White House. Because of all the big dinners and social occasions, Taft's waistline expanded again.

The Tafts also entertained in their home. Will was a gracious host. He did not drink, but he served others as much wine as they wanted. Taft's older brother Charles gave Will and Nellie money to supplement his pay as secretary of war. Otherwise, they could not have afforded to entertain much.

Taft's friendship with President Theodore Roosevelt grew. Taft was to become not only secretary of war, but also a person Roosevelt could send to solve problems all over the world.

The War Department was in charge of many things in addition to wars. One of its major projects was the construction of the Panama Canal.

Roosevelt put Taft in charge of the massive job of building a canal to link the Atlantic and Pacific Oceans via the Isthmus of Panama—a narrow strip of land between the oceans. Panama had once been part of Colombia, but Roosevelt had helped support a revolution that created the new nation of Panama. He felt that dealing with the new nation would be easier than dealing with Colombia. Colombia had not cooperated with the United States' efforts to build a canal.

Taft knew little about Panama. But he put his tremendous power to study and learn all details of a situation to work. He needed to learn the politics of Panama, the logistics of moving great amounts of material, and the engineering problems of building a canal. There was also the problem of disease. Yellow fever was a terrible threat to men working on the canal.

Though the United States was determined to build the canal, no one knew exactly how to do it. Should it be a sea-level canal? Or should it have locks to raise and lower the water levels? The problems were enormous. Eventually, because of the cheaper cost, a lock canal was decided upon.

The construction of the Panama Canal was the largest engineering project ever attempted by the United States up to that time. Taft proved to be equal to the task. He chose a talented engineer, George W. Goethels, to supervise the actual construction. Once Goethels was in charge of

Taft's wife, Helen "Nellie" Herron Taft, in 1908. Nellie Taft enjoyed participating in the social life of Washington, D.C., while her husband served as Roosevelt's secretary of war

the work, the construction proceeded smoothly.

Taft also supported Dr. William C. Gorgas, who had been laughed at when he said that yellow fever was carried by mosquitoes. But when the mosquito population was reduced, yellow fever became less common. This was an important step in the canal construction and in medicine.

Taft campaigned for Roosevelt and the Republican ticket during 1904. He traveled the country making speeches on behalf of Republican candidates. He did not like politics, but he became good at it. Both Roosevelt and the Republican Party won resounding victories. Roosevelt, having served more than three years of McKinley's term, was inaugurated as president in his own right in March 1905.

Running the War Department and supervising the Panama Canal construction would have been enough to occupy most men, but Secretary of War Taft had many other duties as well. He was an active member of the president's cabinet, and he discussed national policy with Roosevelt. Taft agreed with Roosevelt on most issues. He too was for "busting" trusts—breaking up the power of monopolies.

During the late 1800s, combinations of industrial companies and railroads formed. These "trusts" controlled entire industries. For example, Standard Oil, owned by John D. Rockefeller, had a near monopoly in the oil industry. There was a feeling that the trusts were too powerful financially. They could control prices and wages. They were also powerful politically. Many senators and congressmen were said to be "owned" by the trusts, and would vote to advance the interests of the trusts, not the people they were elected to serve.

Roosevelt was determined to break up the power of the trusts. To do this, he used new laws that made monopolies illegal. Roosevelt earned a reputation as a "trust buster." Taft was not directly involved in the trust busting, but he agreed with it. In the congressional elections of 1906 he again campaigned for the Republican ticket.

During this time, he began complaining of becoming sleepy. It was no wonder—his weight had reach 326 pounds. Taft went on a diet. By March 1906, through diet and exercise, he had lost 75 pounds. He got down to 250 pounds by the summer. Because he was a big man, 250 was a good weight for him. He continued to struggle with his weight, though, and he steadily put the pounds back on.

During his time as secretary of war, Taft also made numerous trips as a troubleshooter. One important mission was to Cuba. Unlike the Philippines, Cuba had been given its independence shortly after the United States helped liberate it from Spain. But Congress had insisted on a clause in the Cuban constitution that said the United States

Secretary of War Taft opposed the corruption of political bosses and machine politics in his native Cincinnati.

Taft rides with Alice Roosevelt, daughter of President Roosevelt, and Japanese officials during a diplomatic mission to Japan.

could intervene in Cuba if its stability was threatened. This happened in 1906 when a revolution broke out between feuding Cuban factions, and the Cuban government asked for U.S. assistance.

The United States had to do something, but no one knew just what. Roosevelt sent Taft to Cuba to deal with the situation. Taft landed in Havana in September 1906. American troops landed with him. Both sides had declared a truce in the fighting, and both sides welcomed American intervention. They recognized Taft as a fair and neutral judge of their differences.

For a brief time, Taft acted as provisional governor of Cuba. Peace was restored, and the Cuban government continued to function under Taft's general supervision. Taft returned to Washington, D.C. in October 1906, and a new governor was named. U.S. troops remained to stabilize the Cuban government until 1909.

In 1905 and 1907 Taft made two diplomatic trips to the Philippines. He checked on the country and visited his friends there. A number of U.S. congressmen accompanied him on the 1905 trip in order to see the progress that had been made in the Philippines. During both his 1905 and 1907 trips, Taft also made diplomatic visits to Japan on behalf of President Roosevelt, who wished to convey his respects. The Japan stop became more than a courtesy, however.

In Japan, Taft conducted extensive conversations with the prime minister Katsura, whom he had met during his first visit to Japan in 1903. The outcome of these conversations was the Taft-Katsura Memorandum. It was not a formal agreement. It was just a statement of the positions of the two countries concerning the affairs of the Far East. But it was an important accomplishment. After Taft cabled the statement to Washington, Roosevelt cabled back that he approved "every word."[1]

During his 1907 visit to Japan, Taft addressed a delicate issue. Relations between the United States and Japan had become strained, partly because the school board in San Francisco, California, had decided to segregate Japanese children there into separate schools. Many people in California were prejudiced against Asian immigrants. The school board's decision insulted the Japanese government. Roosevelt sent Taft to Japan to try to make amends. He convinced the Japanese that the United States considered Japan as an equal nation, despite the incident in San Francisco.

Taft's 1907 trip was truly an around-the-world journey.

Charlie, who was then eleven, accompanied his parents on the adventure. From Japan, the family sailed to the Philippines, then to Vladivostock in Siberia, across Siberia by train to Moscow and St. Petersburg, Russia, (where Taft's father had once been the U.S. minister), and then to Berlin and Hamburg, Germany, where they sailed for home. They had traveled 24,000 miles.

Taft's official trips out of the country were many and long, and travel in those days was slow going by rail and by ship. During his four years as secretary of war, he spent 255 days out of the country.[2] On most trips, he took Nellie and one or two of the children. Some newspapers questioned his huge travel expenses. Roosevelt was concerned about the public perception, and he asked Taft to have his wealthy brother Charlie fund the trips. Charlie was happy to help, even though he was already giving his brother a great deal of money for his Washington expenses. Today it is difficult to imagine anyone finding fault with a cabinet officer for traveling the world as a representative of the president.

By the time the Tafts returned from their worldwide trip in 1907, people were seriously talking about William Howard Taft as the Republican candidate for president in 1908. The newspapers liked him. They praised his service in the Philippines, his role in the construction of the Panama Canal, and his diplomatic missions overseas.

Roosevelt could have run again, but he had earlier pledged that he would not seek a third term. No American president had ever served more than two four-year terms. Because Roosevelt had served three years after he took over for McKinley, and then been elected to a four-year term, he said that another four years would violate the

SOURCE DOCUMENT

WAR DEPARTMENT
WASHINGTON

January 1, 1908.

My dear Mr. Graham Bell:

I beg to acknowledge receipt of your volume entitled "The Mechanism of Speech", which you were good enough to have sent me, and to thank you for the same.   I shall have pleasure in looking it over.

Very sincerely yours,

Prof. Alexander Graham Bell,
1331 Connecticut Avenue,
City.

Secretary of War Taft was in touch with Alexander Graham Bell, the inventor of the telephone. Bell continued to experiment with communication throughout his life, later inventing the photophone transmission of sound on a beam of light, the precursor of fiber-optics.

unwritten rule that presidents only served for a total of eight years.

Roosevelt and Taft had become friends. Their sons, Quentin Roosevelt and Charlie Taft, were also friends, and they played together in and around the White House. But Secretary of War Taft's friendship with President Roosevelt was more official than personal. They were different personalities. Taft was quiet and reserved. He was a thinker. Partly because of his size, he was not a big fan of exercise. Roosevelt was a doer. He was an outdoorsman and a fanatic for exercise and the strenuous life. What they had in common was intelligence and background. They both came from well-to-do families. They both believed in the Republican Party. They both agreed that reforms were needed—of business in particular. Taft was the more conservative of the two. Today he might be described as "laid back."

Taft and Roosevelt got along well, and Taft carried out every mission Roosevelt assigned to him. He enjoyed the relationship, as did Roosevelt. It was only natural for Roosevelt to pick his right-hand-man, William Howard Taft, to follow him as president.

7

PRESIDENTIAL CAMPAIGN OF 1908

Taft knew that he might be nominated for president in 1908, but he was not sure he wanted to be president.[1]

He had always wanted to be on the Supreme Court, but his feeling of duty to the Philippines had made him decline the position not once, but twice. Nellie had been happy that he had not gone to the "graveyard" of the Supreme Court bench. She considered it a dull job. She had always felt that her husband should be president. So did his brother Charlie and the rest of the family. Taft allowed his brother Charles to organize a campaign organization to support him. As the Republican convention of 1908 came to a close, Taft finally accepted the nomination, even though he would rather have seen someone else run.

One man who did not support Taft as the Republican

SOURCE DOCUMENT

WM. H. TAFT.

"THE SQUARE DEALER"

This 1908 campaign poster for William Howard Taft identifies him as "The Square Dealer."

candidate for president was Joseph Foraker, former Ohio governor, who had once appointed Taft to the superior court. Now an Ohio senator, Foraker was very powerful. He was a friend of big business, and he opposed Roosevelt's progressive reforms. He thought, correctly, that Taft would continue Roosevelt's policies. Foraker tried to have the Ohio Republican Party oppose Taft's candidacy, but he was no match for the pro-Taft forces. The Ohio Republican Party endorsed Taft anyway.

Foraker was not the only one who feared Taft would continue Roosevelt's business reforms. Even before Taft's nomination, some business people believed that Taft might be too much like Roosevelt. They thought Roosevelt was too much of a reformer. Then the Democratic presidential candidate, William Jennings Bryan, came out for public ownership of the railroads. To business people, this was pure socialism—where the government, not private people, owns the big businesses. Suddenly, Taft was seen as a moderate—especially when compared with Bryan.

Nellie was afraid that Roosevelt would back out of his pledge not to run again and allow himself to be drafted for president by the convention. This could have happened. When Theodore Roosevelt's name was first mentioned at the 1908 Republican convention in Chicago, a forty-five-minute demonstration broke out. The people started chanting "Four more years!" Only when Roosevelt sent word that he was not available did the crowd calm down.

When it became clear that Roosevelt would not run, William Howard Taft was easily nominated on the first ballot. With Taft taking no part in the selection process (as was the custom then), the convention chose James

Sherman, a lackluster conservative senator from New York, as the vice-presidential candidate. It was a bad choice. Sherman was against the progressive reforms that Roosevelt, and now Taft, championed.

Taft disliked campaigning, and he did not look forward to the next four months. In order to devote full time to the campaign effort, Taft resigned as secretary of war. His 1908 campaign for the presidency officially began at his brother Charles's mansion in Cincinnati.

Because he was Theodore Roosevelt's chosen successor, Taft was seen as the candidate of the Progressive Republicans. This was the part of the party that wanted business reform. But the conservative wing of the party also supported Taft. They thought at least he would not be as bad as the Democrat's nominee, William Jennings Bryan.

William Jennings Bryan had run for the presidency twice before, in 1900 and 1896. He had lost both times. The Democratic Party was not strong. The Republicans had the support of most business interests, farmers, small town dwellers, and small shop owners. The strength of the Democratic Party was in the big cities, among immigrants, and among white people in the South, many of whom still blamed the Republican Party for the Civil War.

Taft, with Roosevelt's support, was favored to win the election. Since there were no opinion polls, though, no one could be sure what the people were thinking.

Though Taft would have liked to stay in Cincinnati for the campaign, he agreed to go out "on the stump" and give speeches throughout the nation. Will Taft had never become a great speaker. His speeches were too long and sometimes over the heads of his audiences. But people

William Jennings Bryan was Taft's Democratic opponent in the election of 1908. Unlike Taft, Bryan was an eloquent speaker

liked him anyway. They could see that he was honest and straightforward. He also had an infectious chuckle. He would laugh, and the crowd would laugh with him.

There were three major issues in the presidential campaign of 1908: 1) business regulation, 2) tariffs (taxes on imported goods), and 3) banking.

Roosevelt had already started a plan of regulating industries and "busting" trusts, or making them break up into smaller companies. This was so the smaller companies, when forced to compete against each other, would not be able to control wages and prices like many of the large companies had. Taft promised to carry on Roosevelt's business reforms.

Tariffs had always been a big issue in national politics. For much of its existence, the federal government was able to pay its expenses with these taxes charged on imported goods.

Tariffs had another side, however. They also protected U.S. manufacturing interests. Some goods cost more to produce in the United States than they did in other countries. This was mainly because American workers earned higher wages. American manufacturers wanted protection from an influx of foreign goods. They wanted the government to charge a high tariff on goods from other countries so consumers would buy American goods instead.

On the other hand, producers of raw materials, like cotton, wanted low tariffs. This was because they sold their raw materials overseas, and they wanted other countries not to charge high tariffs on their goods. If the United States charged high rates on goods coming into the country, other countries would do the same, making raw materials hard to sell overseas.

Higher tariffs meant higher prices for consumers, because the tax would have to be added to the final cost of the product. But manufacturers said if tariffs were too low, they would go out of business, causing many working people to lose their jobs.

The Republican Party tended to be on the side of high tariffs. Taft was no exception, but he wanted the tariffs to reflect only the actual difference between American manufacturers' costs and that of other countries. If the tariff were any higher than that, it would not make things equal; it would give an unfair advantage to American business, and cost American consumers more. The issue did not have an easy solution, but Taft promised to "reform" the tariffs. The promise would prove to be easier than its fulfillment.

Banking, too, had always been an issue in American politics. Today, the federal government guarantees that most people will not lose their money if a bank fails and goes out of business. In 1908, there were no such government guarantees. If you put your money in a bank, and the bank went broke, you lost your money.

The Democrats proposed a government system that would tax banks and pay that tax into a kind of insurance fund. If a bank failed, the insurance fund could pay back the bank's depositors. Both Taft and Roosevelt thought this idea would result in ruin because the strong, well-managed banks would have to bail out the weak and badly-run ones. In order for such a system to work, Taft said, the banks would have to be heavily regulated by the government.

Instead of federal regulation of banks, the Republicans proposed a postal bank, managed through the post office,

Taft loved to play golf, and his critics drew attention to this fact, calling it a "rich man's game" and inferring that Taft was aligned with society's elite, not the average working person.

where small depositors' money would be guaranteed by the federal government.

Three more minor issues surfaced during Taft's 1908 campaign: golf, prohibition, and religion.

Taft loved to play golf. It took his mind away from his troubles. Plus, it was about the only exercise he got. Many people thought golf was a rich person's game. This was partly because golf was usually played at private country clubs, where "common" people were not allowed. Theodore Roosevelt liked to play tennis, which had the same elite reputation, but he never let himself be photographed in a tennis outfit. There were many pictures of Taft playing golf, and Taft's weight made him look somewhat comical playing golf.

In the early twentieth century some people advocated "prohibition," or making all alcoholic beverages—beer, wine, and liquor—illegal in the United States. This movement was also called "temperance," which actually means drinking modestly. But the temperance people weren't for drinking in moderation. They wanted to ban alcohol outright. Temperance advocates felt that alcohol was harmful. They pointed to public drunkenness, health problems, and people spending money for drink instead of taking care of their families. Other people thought that prohibition of alcohol was not necessary because most people did not abuse it. They also thought that banning alcohol would lead to smuggling, crime, and "bootlegging" (people making their own liquor).

Taft refused to favor prohibition. While he rarely drank any alcohol, he believed that a prohibition law was a mistake.[2] In hindsight, he was right. Prohibition was tried and later repealed because it was a dismal failure.

Taft casts his vote in the presidential election of 1908. Taft defeated William Jennings Bryan with 51.6 percent of the popular vote to Bryan's 43.1 percent.

Another campaign issue was religion. Most Americans at that time were Protestants. Many were suspicious of other religions. William Howard Taft was a Unitarian. He believed in God, but not in the divinity of Jesus Christ. Although it was not widely known, he was attacked for this view. Strangely, he was also accused of being a Roman Catholic. At the time, some Americans were prejudiced against Roman Catholics. Rumors spread, saying that when Taft dealt with the Pope while governor of the Philippines, he was too "easy" on the Catholics.

While many of these issues were important, the most important feature in the election was that people knew Taft was Theodore Roosevelt's chosen successor. Roosevelt was very popular, and his support helped ensure Taft's victory.

In November of 1908, William Howard Taft was elected the twenty-seventh president of the United States. The vote was not close: 7,675,320 for Taft; 6,412,294 for Bryan. Taft won in all but three states.

Now William Howard Taft was president, the office Nellie always thought he should have, and they would live in the White House.

Will Taft would also have to govern the country.

IN THE WHITE HOUSE

illiam Howard Taft took office as president on March 4, 1909. It was a cold and stormy day. His sense of humor came out when he remarked that he had always said, "It would be a cold day in hell if I get to be president."[1] Taft would later find out that the presidency could be something like hell.

From the beginning, Taft faced a difficult assignment. Theodore Roosevelt had been immensely popular. Roosevelt was a master politician and a great public speaker. He was able to "sell" his programs to the people. Taft hated politics. He was not a great speaker. Most importantly, his nature did not allow him to "go to the people" to rally the nation behind his proposals. He preferred to work through channels.

In choosing his cabinet members, Taft had kept two of Roosevelt's officers. Five of the seven new men were

It was a cold day when Taft, the nation's twenty-seventh president, delivered his inaugural address on March 4, 1909.

lawyers. The Progressive Republicans felt that too many of Taft's cabinet officers were from the conservative wing of the party.

During the campaign, Taft had said that he would follow Roosevelt's progressive policies. He had also said that he would take a break from introducing any new programs. That was so he could work to improve the machinery of government to carry out the reforms already in place. Roosevelt was a thinker and a doer who had rushed into reform. Taft was seen as a detail person—someone who could make the reforms work. Because the reforms required new laws, Taft appointed many lawyers to his cabinet.

In his inaugural address, Taft had spoken of black Americans. He said, "Their ancestors came here years ago against their will, and this is their only country and only flag. They have shown themselves anxious to live for it and to die for it."[2] He promised to be a moderate, but progressive president. He wanted to continue Roosevelt's reform by making the government more efficient.

Nellie Taft loved living in the White House. Ever since visiting there as a teenager, she had wanted to be First Lady. Now she had accomplished her dream. Nellie ran the family part of the White House. She supervised the dinners and parties. There were twice as many dinners as the Roosevelts had given. Nellie also started the tradition of having entertainment after White House dinners. She arranged music performances for the guests.

Will was a gracious host. He did not drink, but he poured much wine for others. He was a warm-hearted man. He laughed and told jokes. One problem was that he would sometimes nod off to sleep after dinner. He would wake up after a few minutes and continue the conversation where he had left off. He would also fall asleep at concerts and sometimes at cabinet sessions.

The newspapers made fun of Taft for falling asleep so easily. He also managed to get stuck in the White House bathtub once. It took six men to get him out. The newspapers also had fun with that. He then bought a bigger tub for the White House.

Son Robert Alphonso and daughter Helen were in college during the Taft's White House years. Robert graduated from Yale in 1910, continuing the family tradition. Robert then went to Harvard Law School, where he finished first in his class. Helen went to Bryn Mawr and eventually received her doctorate there in 1917. The youngest son, Charles Phelps, was eleven when the Tafts moved into the White House. He spent the next four years there.

Taft continued to confide in Nellie, and she helped and advised him about everything. Tragically, she had a stroke in 1909 and temporarily lost her power of speech. Her recovery took a year. While Nellie was recovering, Will sent for their daughter Helen, who took a year off from college and filled in as hostess for White House functions. But Will Taft was without Nellie's advice and counsel. He was alone and depressed. He nursed her back to health. After about a year, she recovered fully.

Despite his success as a judge, administrator, and diplomat, Taft did not feel comfortable as president. His dream had always been to be on the Supreme Court. He had the mind of a judge, not a leader. He was successful in the Philippines, but there he was like a king—whatever he decided was ordered. Here, he had to deal with Congress, the newspapers, and public opinion.

Taft's honeymoon period in the presidency was brief. The Republican Party was bitterly divided. The western and midwestern Progressives hoped that Roosevelt's reforms were just a beginning. The eastern Conservatives, however, believed the reforms had gone too far. The progressive and conservative wings of the Republican Party continued to battle each other during Taft's entire term.

The issues facing the country were difficult. The first to require action was tariff reform. Taft had promised tariff reform in the election campaign. To make good on his campaign promise, Taft called a special session of Congress. This session was to deal solely with tariffs. Taft wanted a careful study of the tariff on each type of goods, followed by a reduction in the rate if that could be justified.

Eastern manufacturing interests wanted to keep tariffs high. That gave them an advantage over foreign goods. They had powerful allies in Congress. Senator Nelson Aldrich of Rhode Island was an advocate of high tariffs.

The bathtub President Taft used in the White House was so large, four workers fit comfortably inside of it.

Along with Congressman Sereno Payne, he was able to keep the tariffs mostly high, while granting some modest reductions. The resulting law, signed by Taft in August 1909, was called the Payne-Aldrich Act.

There were some good features of the Payne-Aldrich Act. Taft got reduced rates for items coming into the United States from the Philippines. That made those goods cheaper here, thus more competitive. The act also created a Tariff Commission. Taft hoped that the commission would study rates and recommend more reductions. Even Theodore Roosevelt said that Taft had done the best he could. But the Progressive Republicans thought Taft had sold out to the high-tariff forces. Consumers got very little by way of reductions on everyday items, and Progressives had wanted a decrease in the cost of living for common people. They also said that the Tariff Commission, while a good idea, would take years to recommend new reductions.

The Payne-Aldrich Act was the beginning of a spilt between Taft and the Progressives. The Conservatives did not like the bill either, which isolated Taft even more. Taft, hating politics as he always had, had tried to do the right thing, only to be whipsawed between two factions that were each very politically adept. He was not good at the game of politics—the give and take among different sides.[3]

Yet Taft was able to make some progressive reforms during the first part of his term. During the campaign, the Republican Party platform had promised to create a postal savings system, a savings bank run by the U.S. Post Office. Because it would be guaranteed by the government, small savers could feel that their money was safe. Taft managed to get Congress to establish the system, despite the opposition of the banks.

The post office itself was in need of reform, and Taft was also able to push efficiency in the post office's operation. The result was that the post office went from a deficit of $17 million in 1909 to a small surplus in the last year of Taft's presidency.[4]

But the reform of the post office also came at a cost to Taft. To make the post office profitable, Taft had proposed that the rates for carrying newspapers and magazines be raised to cover the actual cost of delivery. (Previously, the government had carried them at a substantial loss.) The raise in the postal rate angered the newspaper and magazine publishers. The anger showed in their unfavorable coverage of Taft's presidency.

Taft also supported more regulation of the railroads. The railroads were the major means of transportation, and if the government did not supervise them, they could charge anything they wanted. But his bill did not satisfy the Progressives, who thought it did not go far enough.

To relieve the stress of the presidency, Taft went horseback riding almost every day. He also continued to play golf regularly, despite criticism that it was a "rich man's game." He also liked a new invention, the automobile. Taft had the first presidential automobile—previous presidents had always had horse-drawn carriages.

Taft was the first U.S. president to have a presidential car, shown here.

Another issue that confronted Taft was conservation. Conservation was new to Americans. Since the settling of the country, there had been ample resources. Most of the country had been wilderness. Americans had moved westward from the east coast. Farmers had cleared land by removing vast forests. Oil and coal had always seemed abundant until the industrial age. But by the late 1800s, factories and railroads used a lot more coal and oil than farms and wagon trails ever had. With the industrial age upon them, Americans began to realize they might have to make their resources last. Former President Roosevelt had made conservation of the nation's resources—forests, wilderness, coal, oil, and water—a major goal of his administration. Taft had vowed to carry on Roosevelt's policies.

In 1891, Congress had authorized the president to set aside forests. Later the Interior Department was empowered to regulate these lands.[5] Roosevelt had been

SOURCE DOCUMENT

1678   PROCLAMATIONS, 1911.

April 1. 1911.   BY THE PRESIDENT OF THE UNITED STATES OF AMERICA

A PROCLAMATION

Santa Rosa National Forest, Nev. Preamble.   WHEREAS the public lands in the State of Nevada, which are hereinafter indicated, are in part covered with timber, and it appears that the public good will be promoted by utilizing said lands as a National Forest;

National forest, Nevada. Vol. 26, p. 1103.   Now, therefore, I, William H. Taft, President of the United States of America, by virtue of the power in me vested by section twenty-four of the Act of Congress, approved March third, eighteen hundred and ninety-one, entitled "An Act To repeal timber-culture laws, and for other purposes," do proclaim that there are hereby reserved from settlement or entry and set apart as a public reservation, for the use and benefit of the people, all the tracts of land, in the State of Nevada, shown as the Santa Rosa National Forest on the diagram forming a part hereof.

Prior rights not affected.   The withdrawal made by this proclamation shall, as to all lands which are at this date legally appropriated under the public land laws or reserved for any public purpose, be subject to, and shall not interfere with or defeat legal rights under such appropriation, nor prevent the use for such public purpose of lands so reserved, so long as such appropriation is legally maintained, or such reservation remains in force.

IN WITNESS WHEREOF, I have hereunto set my hand and caused the seal of the United States to be affixed.

Done at the City of Washington this first day of April, in the year of our Lord one thousand nine hundred and eleven, and of [SEAL.]   the Independence of the United States the one hundred and thirty-fifth.

WM H TAFT

By the President:
   P C KNOX
     Secretary of State.

Taft issued this proclamation to set aside public land in Nevada as a National Forest. Like his predecessor, Roosevelt, Taft was a friend of conservation.

a champion of the conservation movement, and it was popular with the public. Gifford Pinchot was Chief Forester under Roosevelt, who had supported his efforts to conserve the nation's forests. Roosevelt had "stretched" whatever legal authority he had to push his conservation crusade. He had used executive orders to withdraw public lands from sale, instead of having Congress pass legislation to do so. Taft disagreed with these tactics. He believed that Roosevelt should have gone through normal channels.[6] He questioned the legality of some of Roosevelt's actions.

Under Roosevelt, Pinchot, who was technically under the authority of the secretary of agriculture, had acted mostly on his own. Later, when President Taft tried to get Pinchot to work through normal channels, Pinchot took this as an attack on his policies, and he attacked Taft. Taft was forced to fire Pinchot. Roosevelt considered the firing of his friend as a personal slap from Taft.

Taft was a friend to conservation. He wanted to accomplish the same goals as Roosevelt, but he wanted to do it in a regular fashion. This was another of the differences in style between the two men. Roosevelt would charge ahead and attempt to accomplish what he wanted without concern for the obligations imposed by the law. Taft, the former judge, was perhaps too mindful of legal detail.

Before radio and television, newspapers were the main source of news. As secretary of war, Taft had been a favorite of the newspapers. He was friendly toward them, and he was involved in newsworthy activities like the building of the Panama Canal and diplomatic missions to Japan. When Taft entered the White House, however, his relationship with the newspapers soured. Unlike Roosevelt, he kept to himself. He did not often talk with reporters. When the president was not giving out any news, the reporters turned to others—often Taft's enemies—who were willing to talk. As a result, more criticism made its way into the news than positive comment. Taft had no idea how to combat this problem, so he refused to worry about it.[7]

The other large legacy of the Roosevelt years was

SOURCE DOCUMENT

Among the perks of the presidency was the chance to meet with famous people like the Wright brothers, the pioneers of flight, who are shown on either side of President Taft in this 1909 White House photo. The picture includes the signatures of the Wright brothers, the president, and the other people present.

"trust busting." Taft continued this practice. In fact, Taft's administration filed many more lawsuits to break up businesses than did Roosevelt's. Under Taft, the huge Standard Oil Company was forced to split into many smaller companies. Its monopoly over gasoline was ended. Taft also broke up the American Tobacco Trust.

Unfortunately, the Progressive Republicans did not give Taft much credit for his trust-busting lawsuits. One case was even held against him. Some years before,

American financier J. P. Morgan had come to President Roosevelt and informed him that a certain company might be in financial trouble. If it collapsed, Roosevelt was told, a number of stock brokerage companies would also fail. To solve the problem, the United States Steel Corporation could buy the company and guarantee its loans. Roosevelt approved the scheme. It turned out later, though, that the real purpose was to create another trust and stifle competition. Taft filed a lawsuit to break up U.S. Steel. This made Roosevelt look bad for approving it. The action against U.S. Steel, while appropriate, was the final strain in Taft's relationship with Roosevelt.

In foreign policy, the Taft administration became known for "dollar diplomacy," which is diplomacy used to promote the nation's financial or commercial interests abroad. Taft saw the role of the government as helping American businesses expand sales to foreign lands, especially the Orient and Caribbean. This policy was based on Taft's belief that trade would benefit not only American business, but also the people of the less-developed nations. These business relationships fostered mutual understanding and helped to prevent war.

Taft continued the American practice of intervention in nearby countries of the Western Hemisphere. Taft sent marines to Nicaragua to protect American property and citizens when the government there became unstable. He also negotiated a loan for Honduras, on the condition that it accept American supervision of some of its financial affairs. During the Taft presidency, Mexico was in a state of revolution and upheaval. Americans had a lot of investment in Mexico, and many Americans lived there. Taft resisted efforts to intervene in Mexico, favoring peace. He

SOURCE DOCUMENT

A 1904 cartoon depicts the Standard Oil Trust as an octopus whose tentacles are strangling Congress, state legislatures, and taxpayers. President Taft diminished Standard Oil's power by breaking it up into smaller companies.

did, however, mobilize twenty thousand troops, in case intervention might be necessary.

During the Taft presidency, both Arizona and New Mexico were admitted to statehood. The process took two tries because Taft vetoed the states' first constitutions. These state constitutions had provided that the voters could "recall," or remove, judges from office. Taft, a former judge, believed that this would make judges fearful in their rulings. When the states submitted new constitutions without the recall provisions, Taft welcomed both new states into the Union.

Taft, a huge baseball fan, also started the tradition of having the president throw out the first pitch of the baseball season. This was at a game on April 10, 1910, between the Washington Senators and the Philadelphia Athletics. Taft loved baseball, and he attended two dozen games while president.[8]

In the 1910 mid-term elections the Democrats captured control of Congress. This was seen as a defeat for President Taft. Things got worse from then on. President Taft, for all of his administrative talent, lacked the political savvy to unite, or at least mediate between, the warring factions of the Republican Party. His presidency drifted, and he became mired in trouble within his own party. These problems were not of his making, but they were beyond his ability to solve.

Taft was at heart a conservative. He believed in reform but wanted to go slowly. He became closer to the conservative element in the Republican Party. He also tried to take a middle road approach to please both sides. He ended up pleasing neither.

Theodore Roosevelt finally concluded that Taft had abandoned his progressive agenda. The end of their long-time friendship spelled doom for the Taft presidency. Nellie predicted the future in July 1910, when she said:

> Well, I suppose you will have to fight him for the nomination, and if you get it he will defeat you. But it can't be helped. If possible you must not allow him to defeat you for renomination. It does not make much difference about the reelection.[9]

A happier event occurred in 1911 when the Tafts celebrated their silver, or twenty-fifth, wedding anniversary in the White House. There were 3,400 guests. As a girl, Nellie had attended the Hayes's silver anniversary in the White House, and now she enjoyed her own silver anniversary there.

Taft makes a ceremonial pitch in April, 1910. Taft started the presidential tradition of throwing the first pitch of the baseball season.

Not many more happy events were in store. As the time for the presidential election of 1912 grew closer, Theodore Roosevelt inched toward becoming a candidate. Roosevelt, having given Taft the presidency, believed it was his to reclaim.

THE ELECTION
OF 1912

aft never really wanted to be president. His time in office had been mainly unpleasant. His presidency had drifted. The newspapers had made fun of him. All the while, he had tried to do his best. One problem was politics, which he disliked. He said in 1910:

> That is just the trouble with the whole country. It is difficult to find good men who are willing to enter politics through the polls or by appointment, and I believe the trouble is that decent, self-respecting men are unwilling to stand for the criticism and abuse which follow one into office through the sensational press of this country.[1]

The presidential election of 1912 was coming up, and Theodore Roosevelt was challenging Taft for the Republican Party nomination. Progressive Republicans wanted Roosevelt back in the White House. Fearing that Roosevelt had become an enemy to business, the Conservative Republicans sided with Taft.

Taft felt he had to run again. He feared that Roosevelt would be bad for the country because he had become too radical and too anti-business.

Theodore Roosevelt's term as president had lasted seven years. When he left office he was still young—he would be just fifty-three during the campaign of 1912. Roosevelt was just over a year younger than Taft. He was in excellent health; he had told a reporter that he was "fit as a bull moose."[2] Roosevelt felt that Taft had abandoned his progressive reforms and that the only way to put the country back on track was for him to take back the presidency.

In the summer of 1910, Roosevelt made a speaking tour of western states. During that tour, he gave speeches on what he called the "New Nationalism." This was his program for a much stronger federal government that controlled the business interests. Roosevelt said this would give every citizen a "Square Deal," and that wealth should be controlled, lest it enslave the people.

Taft was frightened by this talk. He thought Roosevelt had gone too far. Socialism might result from such radical ideas. Taft felt it was his duty to stop Roosevelt from taking over the country.[3]

The truth, as usual, was somewhere in between. There is no doubt that Roosevelt, while out of office, had become more radical. Not having the constraints of being in office, it is easy to be critical of the government. But it is also true that Taft had been too timid. He had drifted into the camp of the Conservatives, who were mainly puppets of the special interests—big business and wealthy individuals. Wealthy people quite naturally favored the status quo because the current system had made them wealthy. They did not see a need for change.

Roosevelt had attacked the courts—the institution Taft favored above all others. Roosevelt was not a lawyer and had little respect for courts. When he was president, Roosevelt was incensed when the Supreme Court invalidated some of his reforms. He said of Justice Oliver Wendell Holmes, whom he had appointed, "I could carve out of a banana a Judge with more backbone than that!"[4] Taft, on the other hand, put perhaps too much faith in the court system.

The Republican Party's losses in the mid-term elections should have signaled Taft to the outcome of the presidential election. Of the forty-one sitting Republican congressmen who were defeated, all but one were Conservatives.[5] The "Taft" wing of the party had suffered the defeat. The Progressive Republicans were gaining ground, while the Conservatives were losing. But Taft failed to see these warning signs.

Taft made his own speaking tour in 1911. He traveled seventeen thousand miles and gave more than two hundred speeches.[6] His reception was polite. The crowds were large but not enthusiastic.

Roosevelt battled Taft for the Republican nomination. In his favor, Taft had the power of patronage, which is the ability to appoint people to government jobs. As president, Taft had appointed hundreds of people to government jobs, and they were expected to be loyal to him. Many of the delegates to the 1912 convention would be party regulars, dependent upon the president for their jobs.

In 1912, most states did not have primary elections

SOURCE DOCUMENT

BIOGRAPHICAL SKETCHES OF PRESIDENTIAL CANDIDATE

of the Republican Party at the Presidential Primary Election to be held throughout
the State of California on Tuesday, May 14, 1912.

THEODORE ROOSEVELT.

THEODORE ROOSEVELT, born in New York, October 27, 1858, of Dutch and Southern ancestry; boyhood was marked by brave struggle for health, and was strongly influenced by his father's high ideals of service for fellow man. Was graduated from Harvard University in 1880; elected, in 1881, to New York legislature, serving three years, during which he constantly battled for political honesty; headed state delegation to National Republican Convention in 1884. Turned to ranch life in the West for two years; returned to New York in 1886 to become Republican nominee for governor, but was defeated; in 1889 was appointed a United States Civil Service Commissioner, serving six years and accomplishing praiseworthy reforms. In 1895, returned to New York to accept post as Police Commissioner, in which capacity he did notable work. In 1897, was appointed Assistant Secretary of the Navy by President McKinley; as a result of his energetic policy the navy was thoroughly prepared for the war with Spain; eager for service at the front, he organized the "Rough Rider" regiment, and with it was in the thick of hostilities in Cuba, finally leading it in the famous charge at San Juan. Elected Governor of New York in 1898, Vice-President in 1900, and became President, on the death of McKinley, in 1901; elected President in 1904, completing the term March 4, 1909. Roosevelt's greatest material achievement while President was as "the man who gave us the Panama Canal," California, destined to profit so greatly thereby, owes gratitude to him as much as to any man. More broadly, his crowning accomplishment was the awakening of the national conscience to duties of faithful and honest citizenship, which, ...ed, should be carried into the political, business ...vate life of the country.

WILLIAM HOWARD TAFT.

WILLIAM HOWARD TAFT, born September 15, 1857, at Cincinnati, Ohio, son of Alphonso and Louise Torrey Taft; married at Cincinnati, June 19, 1886, to Helen Herron, daughter of John W. Herron, of Cincinnati; they have three children, two sons and daughter. President Taft was educated in the public schools of Cincinnati, including Woodward High School, where he graduated in 1874; he graduated from Yale University in 1878, with degree B. A.; the same year he matriculated at the Cincinnati College of Law, graduating in 1880 with degree B. L.; admitted to the bar of the Supreme Court of Ohio, May, 1880; January, 1881, appointed Assistant Prosecuting Attorney; resigned March, 1882, to become Collector of Internal Revenue for the First District of Ohio; resigned following year to enter practice of law, and continued in practice until 1887, holding meantime, from January, 1885, office of Assistant County Solicitor of Hamilton County. In March, 1887, Governor Foraker appointed him judge of the Superior Court of Cincinnati; following year was elected to succeed himself for five years; resigned February, 1890, to accept appointment as Solicitor General of the United States, at hands of President Harrison, being in March, 1892, appointed a judge of the United States Circuit Court for the Sixth Judicial Circuit, and ex officio member of Circuit Court of Appeals; in 1896 became professor and dean of law department of the University of Cincinnati, resigning both judgeship and deanship March, 1900, to accept appointment by President McKinley, as President of United States Philippine Commission. On July 4, 1901, President McKinley appointed him first Civil Governor of Philippine Islands; February 1, 1904, became Secretary of War in President Roosevelt's Cabinet; June, 1908, nominated by Republican National Convention at Chicago for the Presidency, and ...ted ...ivin ...391 ...ed ....to ...169 ...for Bryan

ROBERT MARION LA FOLLE

ROBERT MARION LA FOLLETTE is now in seventh year, in the prime of physical and i manhood. To-day, as always, he fights in of the nameless common people. Whether or hate him, no human being ever doubted devotion to the welfare of the masses. In ing there are no steel, harvester, or oth among his managers and campaign contri representative of predatory interests. Hi past may be expressed in one word— "There she stands. She speaks for herse laws are so many monuments to his geniu structive statesmanship, which does equal rich and poor. Public utility companies dividends, yet give the people better servi cost. Farmers, workingmen, and business all found adequate protection in these la consin stands unfalteringly behind him, a in that dark hour when he was deserted by or faint-hearted representatives of the p cause. America is confronted by grave La Follette alone, among presidential c knows the way. He will crush unlawful m necessaries of life, which is now crushing t by wise regulation, if possible; by having compete with the trusts, if necessary. monopoly is intolerable and shall not endu solution of Alaska's problem; government plied by government railroad and steamship at actual cost; his program for assuring full benefits of Panama Canal; splendid fi ernment steamships on both oceans. No will assure the free highway of the seas. La Follette is a vote to give the balance the National Convention to the man is to the plain people, and whose ...

Three candidates sought the Republican nomination in 1912: Roosevelt, Taft, and Progressive Senator Robert La Follette.

for president, as almost all do now. Instead, they had state conventions, with party regulars choosing the delegates to the national convention. Because of his control of the government, Taft got most of the delegates in the convention states. Thirteen states had "preference" primaries, meaning that voters got to vote for their preference of individuals for the presidency. But even in most of those states, the results of the preference primary were not binding on the delegates. In the primary states, though, the result was terrible for Taft. He got a total of 74,716 votes, while Roosevelt got 1,151,397.[7]

Roosevelt was obviously more popular with the people, but Taft easily won the party's nomination at the Republican convention in Chicago. The Conservatives might have been out of favor with the people, but they controlled the Republican Party machinery. Taft was nominated on the first ballot. William Howard Taft was again the nominee of the Republican Party for president of the United States.

All through the convention, the Roosevelt forces charged that the Taft side had "stolen" delegates. They said that some state conventions were tainted by fraud. The evidence shows otherwise.[8] Politics, especially back then, was not perfect. Cheating abounded on both sides, as it always had. But the cries of "fraud" and "theft" were only to justify what Theodore Roosevelt had begun to think—that he should leave the Republican Party if he was not nominated.

Some of the delegates who favored Roosevelt left the convention and held their own meeting. That meeting called for a new political party—the Progressive Party. It held a separate convention in Chicago, on August 5, 1912, and nominated Roosevelt for president. The new Progressive Party became known as the Bull Moose Party, because of Theodore Roosevelt's statement that he was "fit as a bull moose."

Some supporters told Roosevelt that a third party was a mistake—that Taft and Roosevelt would both lose to the Democratic candidate, Woodrow Wilson. Roosevelt refused to listen. Taft had won the Republican nomination, but once Roosevelt entered the race as a third-party candidate, he was doomed. Roosevelt was likely to split the Republican vote, allowing Wilson to win.

The Democrats and Progressives both had reform platforms. Taft was clearly the candidate of the "old guard" of

Woodrow Wilson, the Democratic candidate, defeated both Taft and Roosevelt to win the election of 1912. Wilson is shown here with outgoing President Taft on Inauguration Day, March 4, 1913.

the Republican Party. While business interests favored Taft, they held back giving money. They were so afraid of a Roosevelt win that many supported Wilson. They felt that Wilson was the "lesser evil"—that is, he would not be as bad as Roosevelt. And they knew that Taft had little chance.

In a major blunder, Taft refused to campaign. Instead of defending the accomplishments of his administration, he was silent. Yet he had been a fair president and had accomplished much. One biographer, commenting on Taft's record, said "In many ways it was a good one, deserving of explanation and defense. It had been honest, responsible, and moderately Progressive."[9]

But Taft did not talk about the good things he had

done. Instead, he let Wilson and Roosevelt call him a failure. The election came down to a contest between Roosevelt and Wilson. Taft was irrelevant. One noteworthy event during the campaign was when a would-be assassin shot Roosevelt. This was in Milwaukee, where Roosevelt was starting to give a speech. Luckily, the speech was still in his pocket. The fifty-page speech absorbed some of the bullet's force. Roosevelt went on to give his speech before receiving medical attention. Later, the wound and his subsequent hospitalization kept him from campaigning for a time and may have cost him the election.

The election was a disaster for Taft. Wilson won easily. Roosevelt came in second and Taft came in third. The vote in the electoral college, which votes by state and elects the president, was Wilson 435; Roosevelt 88; Taft 8. In the popular vote, Taft got close to 3.5 million votes compared to Wilson's 6 million and Roosevelt's 4 million. Despite being an incumbent—the sitting president—Taft received only 23 percent of the vote. He left office in March of 1913. In a letter to a friend, he wrote, "The closer I get to the inauguration of my successor, the greater relief I feel."[10]

William Howard Taft had never liked the presidency. Now he had to find something new to do.

10

BACK TO
THE LAW

At age fifty-six, William Howard Taft was a former president of the United States. He had been in public service for more than thirty years. He was in his middle years and still in good health.

There is no set job for a former president. Many are much older when they leave office. A few have stayed in politics. John Quincy Adams served in the House of Representatives after he was defeated for reelection. But most former presidents simply lived out their lives as private citizens. Not so with William Howard Taft.

Taft had been happiest as a judge. He probably would have stayed in a judicial career if his wife and others in his family had not urged him into appointive office, and then the presidency. He had always wanted to be on the Supreme Court, but because of his sense of duty and need to finish his job in the Philippines, he had turned down the Supreme Court twice.

For the moment, the Supreme Court was out of the question. As president, Woodrow Wilson had the power to fill any vacancy. Taft was a Republican, and Wilson a Democrat, so Taft could not expect an appointment.

After leaving the White House, Taft decided to go back to Cincinnati and practice law.[1] There was no pension for ex-presidents at this time. He would have to earn a living. The prospect of law practice was not pleasant, though. He felt he might be criticized if he accepted big fees from corporations or others seeking to hire him because of his name only.[2]

Luckily, this dilemma was solved when Taft's alma mater, Yale University, offered him a professorship. Because Taft loved the law and thought teaching it was preferable to practicing, he accepted. The only drawback was that the position would take him back to New Haven, Connecticut, not Cincinnati. After a vacation in Augusta, Georgia, Nellie and Will Taft moved to New Haven.

He taught a class on government to undergraduates and a course or two to law students. The position gave him an opportunity to read, study, teach, and write about the law. It was ideal.

While at Yale, Taft wrote three scholarly books: *Popular Government* (1913), *The Anti-Trust Act and the Supreme Court* (1914), and *The President and His Powers* (1916). All three were the product of his thought and research. He did not even have a research assistant, as most professors do now.

Taft also wrote articles for magazines such as the *Saturday Evening Post* and *Ladies Home Journal*. He was

Former President Taft became a professor of law at Yale University in 1913.

paid handsomely for these articles. He also received a good income from speaking fees.[3]

In 1914 he was asked to run for Congress from Connecticut, but after some consideration, he declined. He had had enough of elections. However, he strongly supported former Supreme Court Justice Charles Evans Hughes, the Republican presidential candidate who ran against Wilson in 1916. Taft had appointed Hughes to the Court in 1910, but Hughes had resigned in order to run for president. Hughes did well, but Wilson was reelected in a close race.

Like most Americans, Taft hoped that America could stay out of World War I. But when America entered the war, Taft accepted President Wilson's offer to be co-chair of the National War Labor Board. The board resolved disputes between workers and companies about wages and working conditions. This was necessary to avoid strikes and maintain the production of essential war goods. Taft's judicial training came in handy again, and the board was praised for its even-handed rulings.

After the war, the peace proved difficult. The Treaty of Versailles, which ended the war, contained President Wilson's project—a League of Nations. The purpose of the League was to end war by settling disputes among nations peaceably. Many Republicans opposed the League because they thought it would limit the United States's freedom to do as it thought best.

Taft, however, was a strong proponent of the League of Nations. He put partisanship and his intense dislike for Wilson aside and campaigned for the League. Because the treaty had to be ratified, or approved, by the U.S. Senate to be effective, Taft toured the country giving speeches in favor of ratification. Taft had been involved a few years before in the League to Enforce Peace, a similar proposal. Taft had also pushed for arbitration treaties when he was president. Arbitration—using a neutral party to decide disputes—was preferable to war in Taft's mind. But the Senate had defeated Taft's proposals. Now it also defeated the League of Nations.

Through his teaching, books, magazine articles, and speechmaking all over the country, Taft's reputation was restored. He became a much-admired ex-president.

In 1920, after eight years had passed with a Democrat in the White House, a Republican, Warren G. Harding of Ohio, was elected president. It seemed Taft might get another chance at the Supreme Court after all.

FINALLY, THE
SUPREME COURT

On December 24, 1920, Taft journeyed to Marion, Ohio, to visit President-elect Warren G. Harding at his home. Over breakfast, they talked about many things. Harding then surprised Taft by asking him whether he would accept appointment to the Supreme Court, should a vacancy arise.

Taft explained that he had always wanted to be on the Court. He also explained why he had twice turned down offers. He also said that because he had been president, he felt he could only accept an appointment as chief justice, not as an associate justice. This was not only pride. The Supreme Court was in need of reform, and Taft felt that only the chief justice would have the power necessary to change things for the better.

Harding said he understood, but he did not commit to naming Taft chief justice. In January, 1921, just a few

Taft in the robe he wore as chief justice of the Supreme Court.

weeks later, Gus Karger, Washington reporter for Taft's brother Charles's *Cincinnati Times-Star,* told Taft that he had made a great impression on Harding.[1] According to Karger, Harding had told U.S. Attorney General Harry M. Daugherty that he intended to appoint Taft as chief justice if the opportunity came up. In March, Harding personally told this to Taft.

In May of 1921, Chief Justice Edgar Douglass White (whom Taft had appointed) died. Harding did not immediately nominate Taft, which caused Taft some apprehension. But on June 30, Harding appointed William Howard Taft as the tenth chief justice of the United States. The Senate confirmed his appointment the very same day, with only four senators voting no. This is surely a contrast with today's often drawn out confirmation process.

Taft became the first person—and, to date, the only person—to serve as president and chief justice—head of the executive and then the judicial branch of government. And as Charles Evans Hughes once said, the chief justice of the United States is "the most important judicial officer in the world."[2]

Will Taft finally achieved his lifelong dream. But he was not content to just achieve it—he wanted to make the Supreme Court—and all the federal courts—work better. He was the perfect person to accomplish judicial reform.

SOURCE DOCUMENT

This cartoon from Puck *illustrates the backlog of cases faced by the U.S. Supreme Court. As chief justice, Taft helped reform the federal judiciary so that cases could be heard faster.*

The federal courts were in a mess. There was a shortage of judges. Cases took years to decide. Taft knew that major changes were needed. As chief justice, he was able to get Congress to pass the first reform of the federal judiciary since the Constitution was enacted in 1789. He gained the power to assign cases to different trial judges, depending on their workload. He also set up committees to update rules of procedure. Both of these reforms were included in the Judges Act of 1922.

Another problem was that the Supreme Court had to take any case that came its way. Taft wanted to limit the Court's jurisdiction to important cases only. He accomplished this with the passage by Congress of the Judges Act of 1925.[3]

Taft testified before Congress in favor of both bills. As

president, he had hated politics and was not good at the game. But as chief justice, he was an excellent advocate for his positions. In judicial and legal affairs, he felt more at home than he had in the presidency.

Taft's decisions on the court were generally conservative. He tended to favor property rights over individual rights. In doing so, he was in tune with most other judges of the day. His colleagues on the Supreme Court usually agreed with him, with the notable exception of Justices Oliver Wendell Holmes and Louis Brandeis, who often dissented, or disagreed with, the Court's decisions. Helped by Taft's good nature, the Court worked smoothly.

Taft sometimes sided with labor. In 1923, for example, he ruled in favor of laws to protect women and children from overwork.

Though Taft did not often agree with Justice Holmes's views on the law, the two men became quite close. Taft viewed Holmes as "charming but unsound" on issues before the court.[4] He came to have the same opinion of Justice Louis Brandeis. Brandeis had given him some trouble in the Pinchot affair, and Taft once considered him a dangerous Socialist. But on the Court, Taft was won over by Brandeis's brilliant mind. He did not often agree with Brandeis, but he liked and respected him.

During Taft's tenure as chief justice, the Supreme Court did not have its own building. The Court heard arguments on cases in the Capitol building. The justices had no offices at all. They worked at their homes. This system was very inefficient.

Taft was able to get Congress to appropriate money for a Supreme Court Building. It was only fitting that a co-equal branch of government have its own building.

A happy William H. Taft and Nellie Taft attend Justice Oliver Wendell Holmes's eighty-fifth birthday party in 1926.

The president had the White House. Congress had the Capitol. The Supreme Court needed a building.

Taft did not live to see the building. Congress finally gave the money in 1929, and the cornerstone was laid by Chief Justice Hughes, Taft's successor, in 1932. The Supreme Court Building stands today as a legacy of Taft's service as chief justice of the United States.

William Howard Taft was chief justice from 1921 until 1930. Though justices are appointed to the Supreme Court for life, Taft's heath began to fail during his service. Too sick to continue his work, he resigned in February 1930. When Taft left, he received this letter signed by all the other members of the Supreme Court:

> We call you Chief Justice still—for we cannot give up the title by which we have known you all these later years and which you have made dear to us. We cannot let you leave us without trying to tell you how dear you have made it. You came to us from achievement in other fields and with the prestige of the illustrious place that you lately had held and you showed us in your new form your voluminous capacity for getting work done, your humor that smoothed the tough places, your golden heart that brought you love from every side and most of all your brethren whose tasks you have made happy and light. We grieve at your illness, but your spirit has given life and impulse that will abide whether you are with us or away.[5]

William Howard Taft died on March 30, 1930, just over two months after his brother Charles, who had helped him so much during his career. Taft was buried in Arlington National Cemetery. His beloved wife Helen "Nell" Herron Taft lived in Washington until her death in 1943. She is buried beside her husband in Arlington.

12

LEGACY

Anyone who has been to Washington, D.C., in the spring had seen the marvelous cherry trees that line the streets. Few know whom to thank, but it was Nellie Taft who was responsible for these beautiful trees. She had admired the cherry trees she and her husband saw when they visited Japan in the early 1900s. When the Tafts were in the White House, the Japanese Emperor sent three thousand cherry trees as a goodwill gift.

There are many other legacies from the Taft administration. The Supreme Court Building stands because Chief Justice Taft insisted that this separate branch of government needed its own building. The Panama Canal was built under Taft's supervision. Taft bought the first automobiles for the White House. He loved to "motor" as they called it then. To forget his cares, he would often have his aide take him for a drive. The Sherman Antitrust Act, which Taft so vigorously enforced, is still used today to keep businesses from becoming monopolies.

Taft could also rightly be called "father of the federal budget." As president, he pressed for each department's budget requests to be submitted to the president before they went to Congress. The president could then decide what the total budget would be. As strange as it seems, that was never done before—the departments all sent their money requests directly to Congress. Because of congressional opposition, Taft did not accomplish this during his administration. But because of Taft's groundwork, President Wilson was able to establish a budget for the federal government in 1920.

Perhaps William Howard Taft's greatest legacy is what he devoted his life to—public service. He served the public his entire life, sometimes at great personal sacrifice. Today a Cincinnati building known as the William

One of William Howard Taft's greatest legacies was his effort to create a Supreme Court building for the nation's highest court. In this 1929 photograph, he and other Supreme Court justices stand before a model of the new Supreme Court building.

Another of Taft's legacies was his role in supervising the construction of the Panama Canal. President Taft is shown inspecting the canal in this 1910 photo.

Howard Taft Law Center houses the Ohio First District Court of Appeals, the Probate Court, and the Prosecutor and Public Defender offices. The building was dedicated by Appellate Judge Mark Painter (the author) in 1997.

Taft would have been content to remain a judge in Cincinnati. But he answered a higher calling. He stepped down as a judge to go halfway around the world to govern the Philippines. He agreed to be president only reluctantly. He tried his best to serve in every capacity.

The Taft family carried on his legacy of public service. Son Robert Taft was a United States senator from Ohio for fourteen years. He contended for the Republican presidential nomination twice. Robert's son, also named Robert, served as a United States senator. His son, also named Robert, was elected governor of Ohio in 1998. William Howard Taft's son Charlie served as Hamilton County (Cincinnati) Prosecutor, ran for Ohio governor, and served for decades on the Cincinnati City Council,

Former President and Chief Justice Taft died on March 30, 1930. This photograph of his funeral procession shows his casket being drawn by horses past the Capitol.

including a term as mayor. Charlie's son, Seth, served as a Cuyahoga County (Cleveland) Commissioner, and was also a candidate for governor of Ohio. Seth's son, Frederick "Rick" Taft, serves on the council in the Cleveland suburb of Pepper Pike. Many other Taft relatives have held, and are holding, public office.

Taft was a great success as governor of the Philippines. He was effective as secretary of war during Roosevelt's administration. He had some successes as president, but fate, and Theodore Roosevelt, denied him a second term.

Taft's greatest success was as chief justice of the Supreme Court. It was the job he had wanted all along, but he had been too busy serving his country in other ways to take it until late in life. He was a man who loved the law.

CHRONOLOGY

1857—William Howard Taft born in Cincinnati on September 15.

1874
–1878—Taft attends Yale University.

1880—Taft takes the bar exam and is admitted to practice law; he graduates from Cincinnati Law School and is appointed assistant prosecuting attorney.

1881—Appointed collector of internal revenue in Cincinnati.

1883—Resigns from internal revenue job; forms law partnership.

1886—Taft marries Helen "Nellie" Herron.

1887—Appointed a superior court judge in Cincinnati.

1888—Elected to a full term on the superior court.

1889—A son, Robert Alphonso Taft, is born.

1890—Appointed solicitor general of the United States. The Tafts move to Washington, D.C. A daughter, Helen Taft, is born.

1892—Appointed to the Sixth U.S. Circuit Court of Appeals. The Tafts move back to Cincinnati.

1896—Taft becomes dean of the University of Cincinnati College of Law.

1897—Another son, Charles Phelps Taft II, is born.

1900—President McKinley appoints Taft as head of the Philippine Commission. The Tafts move to the Philippines.

1901—Becomes governor general of the Philippines.

1904—Appointed secretary of war by President Theodore Roosevelt. The Tafts move from the Philippines back to Washington, D.C.

1905—Makes a diplomatic visit to Japan on behalf of President Roosevelt.

1906—Secretary of War Taft goes to Cuba to settle unrest there.

1907—Makes another diplomatic visit to Japan.

1908—Nominated as the Republican candidate for president; elected the twenty-seventh president of the United States.

1909—Sworn into office as president on March 4. Nellie Taft suffers a stroke.

1910—Taft throws out the first pitch at a baseball game, establishing a long tradition.

1912—Receives the Republican Party nomination for president. Loses the election to Woodrow Wilson.

1913—Taft leaves the office of the presidency and becomes a law professor at Yale University.

1921—Appointed chief justice of the United States Supreme Court by President Warren G. Harding.

1930—Due to poor health, Taft resigns as chief justice and dies in Washington on March 30.

DID YOU KNOW?

Events in Taft's Lifetime

Did you know that brothers Orville and Wilbur Wright, printers and bicycle builders from Ohio, made the first flight in North Carolina in 1903? On the sands of Kittyhawk on December 17, they achieved the first manned, controlled, powered flight after years of trial and error. The subsequent development of air travel shrank the globe, connecting distant people and places.

Did you know that an influenza epidemic—the worst epidemic in recorded history—swept the world from 1918–1919, killing 20–40 million people? In October of 1918, 195,000 Americans died from influenza, making it the deadliest month in the nation's history.

Did you know that the stock market crashed on October 29, 1929, or "Black Tuesday," causing financial panic as stock prices hit record lows and investors lost their money? The crash helped lead to a prolonged downturn in the economy known as the Great Depression, during which the gross national product was cut in half, banks and businesses failed, and Americans lost their jobs and their faith in government and the economy.

CHAPTER NOTES

Chapter 2. Growing Up in Cincinnati
1. David H. Burton, *William Howard Taft: In the Public Service* (Malabar, Florida: Robert E. Krieger Publishing Company, 1986), p. 1.
2. Henry F. Pringle, *The Life and Times of William Howard Taft* (New York: Holt, Rinehart and Winston, 1939), p. 9.
3. Pringle, p. 15.
4. Burton, p. 3.
5. Pringle, p. 28.

Chapter 3. The Young Lawyer
1. Henry F. Pringle, *The Life and Times of William Howard Taft* (New York, Holt, Rinehart and Winston, 1939), p. 36–37.
2. Paolo E. Coletta, *The Presidency of William Howard Taft* (Kansas University Press, 1973), p. 1.
3. Pringle, p. 50.
4. Pringle, p. 48.
5. Coletta, p. 3.
6. Pringle, p. 52.
7. David H. Burton, *William Howard Taft: In the Public Service* (Malabar, Florida: Robert E. Krieger Publishing Company, 1986), p. 11.
8. Pringle, p. 61
9. Burton, p. 12.
10. Pringle, p. 78.
11. Burton, p. 12–13.

Chapter 4. Judge Taft
1. Henry F. Pringle, *The Life and Times of William Howard Taft* (New York, Holt, Rinehart and Winston, 1939), p. 241.
2. Pringle, p. 217.

Chapter 5. Governor of the Philippines
1. Henry F. Pringle, *The Life and Times of William Howard Taft* (New York, Holt, Rinehart and Winston, 1939), p. 236.
2. Pringle, p. 241.

Chapter 6. Secretary of War
1. Henry F. Pringle, *The Life and Times of William Howard Taft* (New York, Holt, Rinehart and Winston, 1939), p. 299.
2. Judith I. Anderson, *William Howard Taft, An Intimate History* (New York: W.W. Norton, 1981), p. 89.

Chapter 7. Presidential Campaign of 1908

1. Henry F. Pringle, *The Life and Times of William Howard Taft* (New York: Holt, Rinehart and Winston, 1939), p. 311.

2. Pringle, p. 861.

Chapter 8. In the White House

1. Franny Taft, *William Howard Taft* (December 6, 2002). Manuscript in possession of the author.

2. Bartleby.com, "Inaugural Addresses of the Presidents of the United States," <http://www.bartleby.com/124/pres43.html> (April 14, 2003).

3. Paolo E. Coletta, *The Presidency of William Howard Taft* ((Kansas University Press, 1973), pp. 45–75.

4. David H. Burton, *William Howard Taft: In the Public Service* (Malabar, Florida: Robert E. Krieger Publishing Company, 1986), pp. 75–76.

5. Coletta, p. 77.

6. Coletta, p. 80.

1. Henry F. Pringle, *The Life and Times of William Howard Taft* (New York: Holt, Rinehart and Winston, 1939), p. 416.

8. *Baseball-Almanac,* "Famous Firsts in Baseball," <http://baseball-almanac.com/firsts/first2.shtml> (April 14, 2003).

9. Archibald Butt, *Taft and Roosevelt: The Intimate Letters of Archie Butt,* (New York: Doubleday, Doran & Company, Inc., 1930), Vol. II, p. 436.

Chapter 9. The Election of 1912

1. Archibald Butt, *Taft and Roosevelt: The Intimate Letters of Archie Butt,* (Garden City, New York, Doubleday, Doran & Company, Inc., 1930), Vol. II, p. 459.

2. White House Web site, "Biography of Theodore Roosevelt," <http://www.whitehouse.gov/history/presidents/tr26.html> (April 14, 2003).

3. Henry F. Pringle, *The Life and Times of William Howard Taft* (New York: Holt, Rinehart and Winston, 1939), p. 764.

4. Henry J. Abraham, *Justices and Presidents: A Political History of Appointments to the Supreme Court* (New York: Oxford University Press, 1992), p. 69.

5. David H. Burton, *William Howard Taft: In the Public Service* (Malabar, Florida: Robert E. Krieger Publishing Company, 1986), p. 102.

6. Paolo E. Coletta, *The Presidency of William Howard Taft* (Kansas University Press, 1973), p. 221

7. Coletta, p. 235.

8. Pringle, p. 806–807.
9. Burton, p.107.
10. Pringle, p. 843.

Chapter 10. Back to the Law
1. Henry F. Pringle, *The Life and Times of William Howard Taft* (New York, Holt, Rinehart and Winston, 1939), p. 847.
2. Ibid.
3. Pringle, pp. 856–57.

Chapter 11. Finally, the Supreme Court
1. Henry F. Pringle, *The Life and Times of William Howard Taft* (New York, Holt, Rinehart and Winston, 1939), p. 956.
2. Pringle, p. 961.
3. David H. Burton, *William Howard Taft: In the Public Service* (Malabar, Florida: Robert E. Krieger Publishing Company, 1986), p. 128.
4. Pringle, p. 969.
5. Burton, p. 141.

Illustration Credits: National Park Service/William Howard Taft National Historic Site, 4, 9, 11, 12, 13, 15, 19, 21, 24, 27, 28, 34, 37, 38, 41, 44, 53, 55, 57, 60, 63, 65, 72, 78, 82, 85, 88, 91, 92, 93.

Source Document Credits: Library of Congress, 47, 66, 70, 76; National Park Service/William Howard Taft National Historic Site, 17, 43, 50, 68, 86.

FURTHER READING

Bromley, Michael L. *William Howard Taft and the First Motoring Presidency 1909–1913*. Jefferson, North Carolina: McFarland and Co., 2003.

Greenberg, Judith E. *Helen Herron Taft: 1861–1943* (Encyclopedia of First Ladies). New York: Children's Press, 2000.

Joseph, Paul. *William Howard Taft*. Edina, Minnesota: Checkerboard Library, 2001.

Maupin, Melissa. *William Howard Taft: Our Twenty-Seventh President*. Chanhassen, Minnesota: Child's World, 2002.

Sandak, Cass R. *The Tafts* (First Families) Mankato, Minnesota: Crestwood House, 1993.

INTERNET ADDRESSES

The Taft Biography from the White House Web Site
  <http://www.whitehouse.gov/history/presidents/wt27.html>

William Howard Taft National Historic Site
  <http://www.nps.gov/wiho>

Internet Public Library Article on Taft
  <http://www.ipl.org/div/potus/whtaft.html>

The American Presidents Web Site
  <http://www.americanpresidents.org>

Taft Biography
  <http://odur.let.rug.nl/~usa/P/wt27/about/taftbio.htm>

PLACES TO VISIT

Ohio
The William Howard Taft National Historic Site, Cincinnati. Located at 2038 Auburn Avenue, the birthplace of William Howard Taft has been restored to its original appearance. A separate building houses exhibits of Taft's life, and of the Taft family. Open year-round. (513) 684-3262.

Washington, D.C.
The White House, 1600 Pennsylvania Avenue. For admission, get tickets in advance from your senator or congressperson, or call the visitor center at (202) 456-7041. Open year-round.

The Supreme Court of the United States, One First Street Northeast. This is the building Taft planned but never got to see. Open 9 A.M. to 4:30 P.M. Monday through Friday except for federal holidays. For tours, call (202) 479-3000.

Connecticut
Museum of American Political Life, West Hartford. Located at 200 Bloomfield Avenue, the Museum of American Political Life at the University of Hartford is devoted the history of presidential campaigns. Open year-round. (860) 768-4090

Virginia
Taft Burial Site, Arlington. Arlington National Cemetery is home to many famous Americans. Open to the public daily from 8 A.M. to 5 P.M. October through March, and 8 A.M. to 7 P.M. April through September. (202) 692-0931. <http://www.arlingtoncemetery.org>.

INDEX

Book Orders

To purchase copies of this or other books in the Ohio Presidents Series, E-mail quantity price and or P.O. order (library and public entities only) inquiries to booksales@cincybooks.com.

For orders, make check payable to Cincinnati Book Publishing, $14.95 per book, plus $1.05 Ohio tax if applicable, and $4 each S&H. Send total of $20 to:

Cincinnati Book Publishing
2449 Fairview Avenue
Cincinnati, OH 45219
http://www.cincybooks.com